Going to have Surgery

A TODDLER PREP™ BOOK

Ready™
SetPrep

About Toddler Prep™ Books

The best way to prepare a child for any new experience is to help them understand what to expect beforehand, according to experts. And while cute illustrations and fictional dialogue might be entertaining, little ones need a more realistic representation to fully understand and prepare for new experiences.

With Toddler Prep™ Books, a series by ReadySetPrep™, you can help your child make a clear connection between expectation and reality for all of life's exciting new firsts. Born from firsthand experience and based on research from leading developmental psychologists, the series was created by Amy and Aaron Pittman – parents of two who know (all too well) the value of preparation for toddlers.

You're going to have surgery. Surgery is when you go to sleep, and a doctor fixes something in your body. Let's talk about what happens when you have surgery.

4

There is a lot to do to get ready! First, we pick out some comfy clothes for you to wear.

Next, we pack a bag of fun toys and games to keep you busy while we wait. What do you want to bring?

Then, we pack your favorite stuffed animal or blanket for you to snuggle.

The night before your surgery, we make sure to go to bed on time so your body is rested and ready.

Sometimes you aren't allowed to eat before surgery. But don't worry, you get to have a special treat when you're all done.

When it's time to go, we drive to the hospital and check in at the front desk.

There might be important papers for me to fill out. You can play with your toys or read a book while you wait patiently.

After I fill out the papers, we wait for your turn in the waiting room.

When it's your turn, a nurse calls your name and takes us to a room.

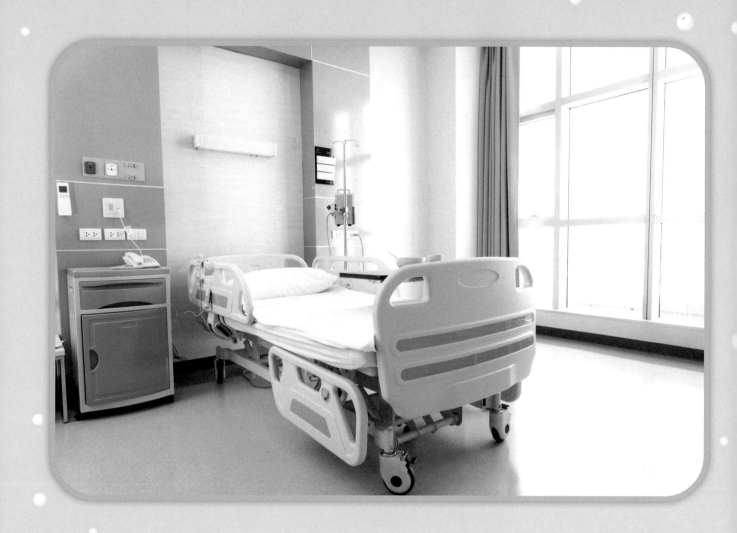

Inside the room, there is a bed for you to lie on and tools for the nurses and doctors to use.

We take off your clothes and put on a special hospital gown. This makes it easy for the doctor to see your body.

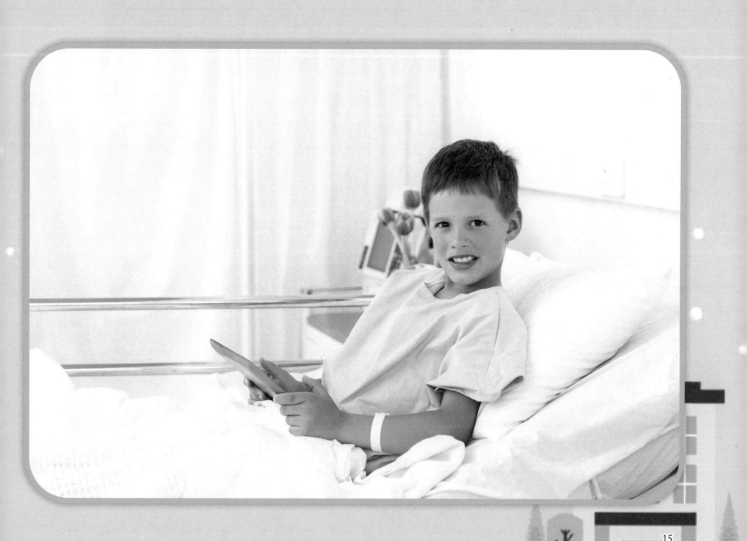

After we put on your gown, the nurse uses a thermometer to check your temperature and a blood pressure cuff to check your blood pressure.

When the nurse is done, the doctor comes in to say hello and ask us some questions.

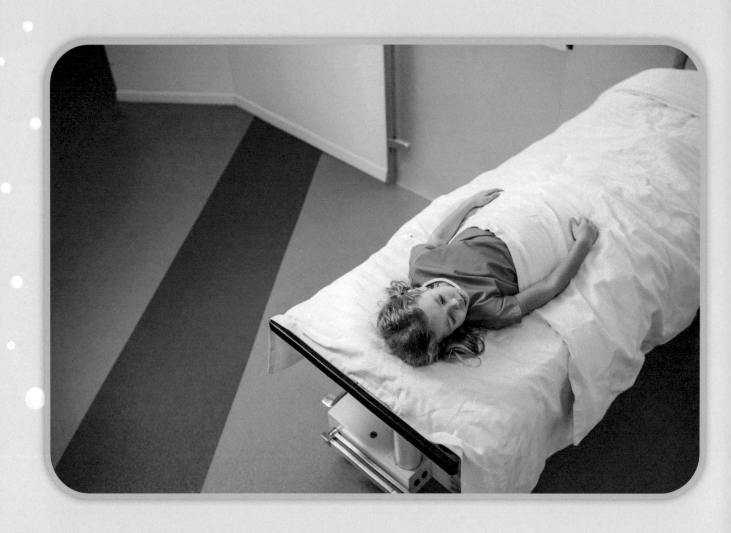

Now it's time for your surgery.
You take a fun ride on a big bed with wheels all the way to the operating room.

The operating room has bright lights and machines that go *beep-beep-beep*.

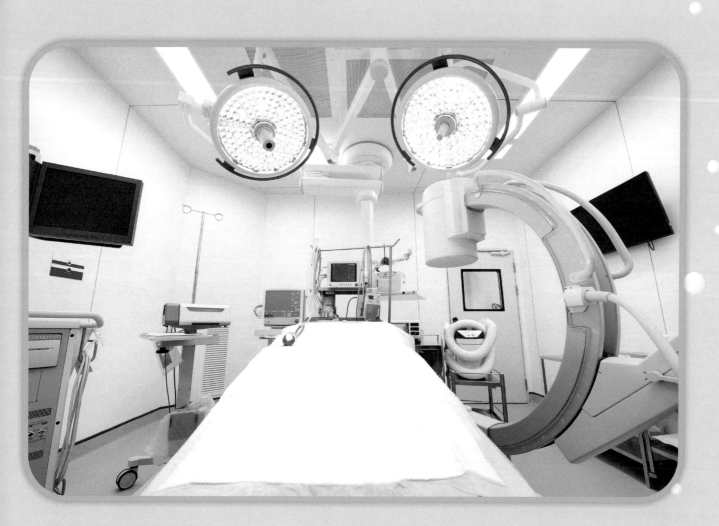

Here, the nurse helps you fall asleep. To fall asleep, you wear a mask on your face, or you play a fun balloon game.

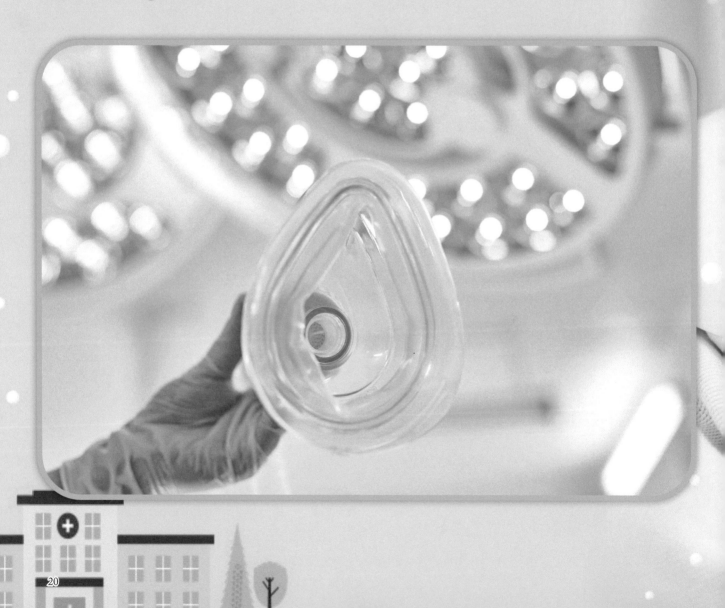

Next, you take a nap while the doctor performs the surgery. I wonder what fun dreams you will have?

Once you wake up, you might feel a little sleepy or grumpy. That's ok. You can rest or cuddle with me.

Then, when you're ready, you get to have a special treat - a juice box or even a popsicle!

Sometimes when you have surgery you spend the night at the hospital. Sometimes you go home right away.

No matter what, I am always with you to take care of you.

You did it! Now it's time to go home and rest.

Made in United States
Cleveland, OH
11 October 2024

10161329R00017